VOLUME

4

FABLES
&
THEIR MORALS

THE ROOSTER AND THE FOX
to
THE WOLF IN SHEEP'S CLOTHING

by

Bruce and Becky Durost Fish

Chelsea House Publishers
Philadelphia

CHELSEA HOUSE PUBLISHERS

Editor in Chief Stephen Reginald
Managing Editor James D. Gallagher
Production Manager Pamela Loos
Art Director Sara Davis
Picture Editor Judy Hasday
Senior Production Editor Lisa Chippendale
Designers Takeshi Takahashi, Keith Trego

First Printing

1 3 5 7 9 8 6 4 2

Library of Congress Cataloging-in-Publication Data

Fish, Bruce.
Fables and their morals / by Bruce and Becky Durost Fish.
    p. cm.
Includes bibliographical references and index.
Summary: Illustrated retelling of one hundred classic fables
from around the world.

ISBN 0-7910-5210-9 (set), 0-7910-5211-7 (vol. 1),
0-7910-5212-5 (vol. 2), 0-7910-5213-3 (vol. 3),
0-7910-5214-1 (vol. 4)
1. Fables. 2. Tales. [1. Fables. 2. Folklore.] I. Fish, Becky
Durost. II. Title.
PZ8.2.F54Fab 1999   98–36355
398.2—dc21   CIP
                                                         AC

CONTENTS

INTRODUCTION

Fables are stories that feature animals with human characteristics. The animals' experiences teach us lessons about life and the way people behave. The word *fable* comes from the Latin word *fabula*, which means "a telling." While the stories usually end with a moral that summarizes what the story is teaching, the emphasis is on the story itself.

Fables are one of the oldest forms of stories. Before it was easy to write things down, they were passed on orally. Parents or wise people in a village would tell the stories to the children, who would grow up and pass the stories on to their children. Originally fables were told as poems because it is easier to memorize words that rhyme and have rhythm than it is to remember prose.

One of the most famous fable writers was Aesop. Many people think he lived in or near Greece during the sixth century B.C. and created about 200 fables. As far as we know, Aesop never wrote down his fables. The first person known to have put Aesop's fables into a collection was Demetrius of Phaleron, who lived in the fourth century B.C.

Aesop's fables have remained popular for 2,600 years, making him one of the most successful figures in the history of literature. His stories spread throughout Greece and Rome. When the Roman Empire expanded as far as Britain, soldiers carried Aesop's stories with them all across what is now Europe. His stories even traveled to Japan. When Jesuit missionaries arrived in Japan during the 16th century, they taught Aesop's fables to the Japanese.

But Aesop's stories are not the only fables we know of from ancient times. Many scholars believe that fables in India date back to the fifth century B.C. They were first used to instruct followers of the Buddha about his teachings. Many of these early stories are called *Jakatas*. They are birth stories about the Buddha and tell some of his experiences when incarnated as different animals, that is, when he was born as various animals. These stories include morals.

Another important group of fables from India is called the *Pancatantra*. The *Pancatantra* was originally written in Sanskrit. The oldest copy of it available is an Arabic translation from the eighth century called the *Kalilah wa Dimnah*. The stories feature two jackals who counsel a lion king. The tales teach political wisdom and cunning. They were translated into many languages, and in the 13th century a Latin version reached Europe.

For centuries, China did not have fables because traditional Chinese thought did not accept the idea of animals thinking and behaving like humans. The Chinese preferred stories based on actual events. But between the fourth and sixth centuries, trade with India made Chinese Buddhists familiar with the Indian fables that helped explain Buddhist teachings. Chinese Buddhists adapted these fables and collected them in the book *Po-Yü ching*.

Japan also has a tradition of fables. Well before Aesop's fables reached Japan, the Japanese had official histories from the first and eighth centuries that featured stories about small, intelligent animals getting the better of big, stupid creatures.

Bernard Binlin Dadié, a 20th-century writer from the Ivory Coast, published several books of African fables and folktales that he collected from that continent's oral traditions. As in other regions of the world, African fables feature animals with human characteristics.

Because of the continuing popularity of fables, many authors have written their own collections. Some fables became quite long. These expanded stories are called *beast epics*. The most famous example of a beast epic is *Roman de*

Renart, written in the 12th century. It contains related stories about Renart the Fox, who represents a cunning man. But most fables are much shorter and in the style of Aesop.

The 12th century also produced a book of short fables by Marie de France, a French poet. Her book was called *Ysopets* and was very popular.

Another French poet, Jean de La Fontaine, published a 12-book collection of fables between 1668 and 1693. Titled *Fables,* these stories are among the greatest masterpieces of French literature. Some experts consider La Fontaine's fables to be the best ever written.

In the late 19th century, publishers began producing many more children's books. Because of this, more authors began using fables in their work. Lewis Carroll (whose real name was Charles Dodgson) released *Alice's Adventures in Wonderland* in 1865. Its animal characters such as the rabbit and the walrus have human qualities. Beatrix Potter self-published *The Tale of Peter Rabbit* in 1900. It was picked up by Frederick Warne and Company in 1902, and the collection of stories about Peter, his family, and Farmer McGregor became one of the best-selling children's books of all time.

Kenneth Grahame's *The Wind in the Willows* with its animal characters Mole, Rat, Badger, and Toad was published in 1908. And Christopher Robin's toy animal friends in *Winnie-the-Pooh* (1926) and *The House at Pooh Corner* (1928), by A. A. Milne, act like human beings and teach lessons about life.

In the 20th century, the use of fable took a darker turn with the publication in 1945 of George Orwell's *Animal Farm.* With the famous line "All animals are equal, but some animals are more equal than others," Orwell's story of animals in a farmyard pilloried Josef Stalin and his oppressive government in the U.S.S.R.

Watership Down, by Richard Adams, and *The Redwall Books,* by Brian Jacques, also draw on the fable tradition. Many science fiction fantasy books, such as J.R.R. Tolkien's

The Hobbit and *The Lord of the Rings* trilogy, use elements of the fable to give a greater sense of reality to the imaginary worlds where they take place.

As new means of storytelling have emerged, the fable has continued to be used effectively. Elements of the fable can be found in comic strips such as *Peanuts,* by Charles Schulz; *The Far Side,* by Gary Larson; and *Shoe,* by Jeff MacNelly. Movies such as *Babe* and *The Lion King* are fables presented through film.

Considering that fables have remained popular for thousands of years, it may only be a matter of time before they are adapted to computer games, virtual reality programs, and other creative avenues yet to be developed.

AESOP

Exactly who Aesop was remains a mystery. Some people think he never existed. They say that Aesop is a legendary figure who was invented to give a name to the anonymous creators of the roughly 200 fables that are attributed to him.

But from ancient times, people have told stories about Aesop and his life. Herodotus, a Greek historian who lived in the fifth century B.C., wrote that Aesop was a slave who lived in the sixth century B.C. Most other stories about Aesop agree that he was a sixth-century slave. One story says that his master Jadmon was so impressed with Aesop's wisdom that he freed the slave.

Stories differ about where Aesop was from. Some say that he was from Thrace, others that he was from Phrygia. An Egyptian biography written in the first century places Aesop as a slave on the island of Samos. Plutarch, a first-century Greek biographer, wrote that Aesop was an adviser to Croesus, the king of Lydia. While the places differ, they all are in or near what is now Greece and Turkey.

After Aesop was freed from slavery, stories tell of him traveling throughout the ancient world, advising rulers and telling stories to both teach and entertain. Some accounts say that Aesop went to the ancient kingdom of Babylon (modern Iran) and became a riddle solver for King Lycurgus.

Another story tells of Aesop visiting Athens and the court of its ruler Peisistratus. He convinced the citizens of Athens to keep Peisistratus as ruler by telling them the fable "The Frogs Who Wanted a King" (see volume 2 of this series).

A 14th-century monk named Maximus Planudes who

admired Aesop's fables described him as an ugly deformed dwarf. Earlier biographers don't mention Aesop's appearance. Many people think that if Aesop were so disfigured, people living closer to his time would have mentioned it.

Herodotus wrote that Aesop died in the Greek city of Delphi, an important religious center. Apparently the citizens became angry with Aesop and threw him off a cliff, but there are several differing accounts of what provoked their attack.

In one story, Croesus, the king of Lydia, sent Aesop as an ambassador to Delphi with a large sum of gold to distribute among the citizens. When Aesop arrived, he was so appalled by the citizens' greed that he refused to give them the gold. Instead he sent the money back to Croesus.

Another writer claims that the people of Delphi were offended by the sarcastic tone of Aesop's fables. Still others suggest that Aesop died as a punishment for embezzling money from Croesus or for stealing a silver cup.

Whatever the truth may be about Aesop's life and death, his stories continue to entertain and enlighten new generations of readers.

THE ROOSTER
AND THE FOX

ne evening a wise old rooster flew up to his accustomed perch on the roof of the hen house. He fluffed his feathers and stamped his feet, settling himself for a long night's rest.

Just then a shadowy form trotted into the farmyard between the hen house and the barn. Even in the fading light, the rooster recognized the distinctive nose, ears, and tail of a notorious local fox. The few chickens still in the farmyard fled at the sight of him.

"I have great news," cried the fox. "The representatives of all the animals of field and forest have joined together in a great treaty of peace. There shall be no more fear of one animal eating another. I myself am pledged to adopt a diet of vegetables, grains, and fruit. Come out and let us all celebrate this historic achievement."

"My word," squawked the rooster. "A treaty of peace between all animals. Is such a thing possible?"

The rooster looked thoughtful and gazed off toward the farmhouse. "Well, well, perhaps it is," he crowed. "I see the farmer's two Great Danes running in our direction. They seem very eager to join in the celebration."

"Two Great Danes, you say?" replied the fox in a shaken voice. "I should really not stay any longer. I have many others to tell of these glad tidings."

"As you wish," replied the rooster, "But I'm sure you will be missing quite a celebration here."

Moral: A cunning creature is no match for a wise one.

THE ROOSTER
AND THE JEWEL

rooster spent his day searching for food. He looked in the barnyard, the garden, and the fields. Finally his search took him to the big grassy front yard of the gray-and-white two-story farmhouse. He knew that somewhere near the giant oak whose branches spread over half the yard he would find the remains of a large lunch that the farmer and his family had shared a few days before with some friends from a nearby town.

As he was scratching in the grass, his talons caught on a thin golden chain made up of small, square links. Suspended from it was a bright red jewel faceted into the shape of a small rectangle.

"What a pretty little bauble," remarked the rooster. "The farmer's eldest daughter often wears something like this around her neck, I believe."

With that, he picked the necklace up in his beak and

flew with it to the front porch of the nearby farmhouse. Carefully, the rooster laid the necklace next to the front door. Then he hopped up on the porch railing and launched himself back out across the lawn in a shallow glide. He landed near the spot where he had discovered the necklace.

"I'm sure the young lady will be glad to have that back," he muttered to himself as he poked at the grass with his beak. "But I would be happier to find some of the food the family dropped while they were eating here."

Moral: A thing of great value to one person is often useless to another.

THE SHEPHERD BOY
AND THE WOLVES

young boy was given an important task by the elders of his village. He was to watch the villagers' sheep and other livestock as they grazed in a large field near the village. At the far side of the field was a dark evergreen forest, and from it wolves sometimes emerged, hungry for meat. The boy had been told to run to the village and get help if the wolves appeared.

One day the young shepherd decided to see what would happen if the villagers thought wolves were attacking. He ran toward the village, shouting, "Wolves! Wolves! There are wolves in the field!"

Everyone in the village dropped whatever they were doing, picked up their weapons, and came running. When they reached the field, they found the boy doubled over with laughter and realized he had tricked them.

Four days later, the boy gave another false alarm. Again he laughed when the villagers came panting to the field.

Two weeks passed quietly. Then one evening, just as the sun was setting behind the forested hills above the field, a real wolf pack crept out from under the trees. They flowed like grey shadows across the pasture, and wherever they went, the flocks scattered in terror. The boy ran screaming for help. Many heard his frantic calls, but everyone ignored them.

Fifty yards from the edge of the village, the young shepherd boy was chased down by two large wolves. They dragged him, still screaming, into the dark embrace of the forest.

Moral: No one believes liars, even when they are telling the truth.

THE SICK
STAG

n the early spring a powerful stag became ill. With the last of his strength, he found a small mountain meadow with plentiful grass and berry-laden bushes that the forest animals had missed. Nearby, clear water flowed from a spring-fed stream. The stag spent hours lying in the tall grass and enjoying the warm sun. With food and water nearby, he could rest safely, and his strength began to return.

Soon his friends began to visit him to check on his progress.

A kindly old black bear was the first to appear. As they talked, the bear noticed the unusually large crop of berries scattered across the meadow. After he had eaten his fill, not many berries were left for the stag.

A few days later, a herd of antelope wandered into the meadow. They asked many questions about the stag's health while chomping large quantities of wild grass.

The very next day, a mountain goat stopped by for a visit. Afterward he clambered around on the rocky ledges that lined one side of the meadow. A loose rock started a landslide that crashed down and buried most of the grass and all the berry bushes. The stream became a rock-strewn muddy mess.

After the dust settled, the stag saw that he would find no more decent food or water there. That night he left quietly to find a new place to recuperate. He was careful not to tell any of his friends where he was going.

Moral: Some who appear to offer you support care about only their own needs.

THE SNAKE
AND THE CRAB

n ocean crab grew tired of listening to the pounding surf and scrabbling to escape the constant danger of being eaten by shore birds. One night he left his tide pool and scuttled across the wide beach, seeking shelter in a field of marsh grass. Daylight found him crawling through the marsh toward a nearby forest of pine, oak, and maple trees.

In the middle of the marsh he met a snake who was also headed for the forest. Over the next several hours they became fast friends. That evening, when they reached the edge of the forest, the snake announced that he was hungry. The crab suggested that they return to the marsh and hunt for frogs, water bugs, and small fish.

"I have something more tasty in mind," replied the snake, as he began to slither toward a tall oak tree. Two finches watched the snake's progress from the nest that held their hatchlings.

The snake called out to them, "Listen, my friends, I have urgent news. There is a hawk circling above us. He is certain to find your nest unless you drive him away."

The finches immediately flew off to look for the intruder.

"Give me a few minutes," hissed the snake, "And we will both feast on tender young meat."

"You can't be serious," replied the crab in disgust. "It's against the laws of nature to capture prey through deceit."

With that the crab scuttled over, grabbed the snake behind the head, and strangled him with his powerful pincers.

Moral: Deceit can be a deadly vice.

THE STAG
AND THE FAWN

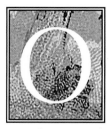ne twilight a fawn saw an old stag racing through a meadow as if all the wolves in the world were after him. The fawn crouched down in the undergrowth and waited to see what was chasing him. When nothing appeared, she crept back down the path the stag had taken, hoping to find the reason for his fear.

About a quarter of a mile from the meadow, she found two dogs playing together in a farmer's field. They were barking furiously as they ran back and forth through the short yellow stubble.

Later that evening, the fawn came across the stag as he was drinking from a deep pool at the edge of a river. She described to him what she had seen and asked, "Is there some new danger in the forest that I should know about?"

"As much as I hate to admit it," replied the stag, "I was

running from two dogs, and I don't even think they were chasing me."

The fawn was amazed. "But you are much larger and stronger and faster than any dog. If they actually caught up with you, your horns and hooves could inflict terrible wounds on them."

"You are right of course, little sister," said the stag sheepishly, "But I have been frightened of dogs since I was your size. Whenever I hear them barking, I feel my life is in great danger, and I cannot keep myself from running away."

Moral: Those who flee in terror do not always understand what they fear.

THE STAG AT
THE POOL

stag stood drinking from a deep, dark pool. He looked at his reflection and admired his large antlers but frowned at the sight of his knobby knees and long, spindly legs.

He sighed with regret. "If only the rest of my body could live up to the fine standard set by my grand and beautiful antlers, then I would be truly happy."

Suddenly a mountain lion burst out of a nearby thicket. The stag reached full speed in less than six strides. Bounding across the stream he slowed to thread a path though several large boulders.

His speed increased again as his hooves dug into the dry forest floor. He soon left the open paths of the pine forest and plunged into a series of deep thickets at the base of a tall rock outcropping.

Without warning his antlers snagged in the crisscrossing branches. The stag spun completely around and lost his foot-

ing. The weight from his twisting body threatened to break his neck. At the last moment, his left antler broke off and the momentum of his fall pulled the remaining horns free.

The stunned animal staggered to his feet and stumbled blindly through a choking cloud of dust. The crashing sounds of pursuit came at him from the right. He turned left and put on a new burst of speed, leaving the mountain lion far behind.

For the rest of his long life, the stag was grateful every day for his swift, spindly legs.

Moral: Do not let vanity blind you to what you need to survive.

THE SWAN
AND THE STORK

swan and a stork spent a lifetime building a close friendship. They were born in the same marsh surrounding a large lake, and they migrated together every year with the change in seasons.

Nothing in all those years had prepared the stork for the distress he felt one fall as he watched his friend. As large flocks of birds began their migration south, he saw the swan struggle to fly high enough to reach his group.

As the moon grew brighter each night, the undulating V-formations of great birds often flew on after sunset. The swan found it easier to fly at night, when the cool air carried the first hint of frost.

On many nights the swan broke into joyous song, and others echoed his calls. The stork wondered where his friend found the energy to sing when he seemed to have barely enough strength to fly.

When they reached the lake where they had enjoyed so many winters, the stork asked the swan, "How is it that your songs have been so joyous during a journey that has been so difficult?"

"I am dying," replied the swan quietly. "I have felt it coming on since last year, but I have not mentioned it, hoping to spare you pain."

"This is awful," replied his friend. "How can you be happy about your death?"

"I am about to enter a place where I will no longer be in danger from snares or guns, predators or hunger. Who would not celebrate such a deliverance?"

Moral: Learn to embrace what you cannot avoid.

The Thief and the House Dog

or weeks a thief had been watching the old manor house at the edge of a town. He had heard in a pub that the man who lived there, a lord, was still wealthy, even though he had given away most of his land so the town could be built on it. More important still, everyone said that the lord lived in the big house with only his wife, a housekeeper, and a Great Dane named Toby.

One Friday night, when the thief saw that the house was dark, he crept to one of the rear windows and began to open it. He was annoyed to find, after all his careful planning, that Toby had been left home. Soon the dog appeared in a walled courtyard, just around the corner from where the thief was working. Worse than that, he started barking, and Toby's bark was loud enough to wake the dead.

To quiet the dog, the thief threw several thick slices of

roast beef over the wall into the courtyard. Though he hadn't expected the dog, he had come prepared for any emergency.

To his great surprise, the dog merely sniffed at the meat and then addressed him in good English. "When I first saw you, I thought you might be a thief, and now I find that my suspicions are confirmed because of your bribe. If you don't leave immediately, I'll jump this wall and tear you to pieces."

Moral: A ready bribe always betrays the presence of a thief.

THE TOWN MOUSE AND THE COUNTRY MOUSE

town mouse once visited a friend who lived in the country. The country mouse served her friend from town a lunch of corn kernels, dandelion greens, wheat stalks, and fresh strawberries in spring water. The town mouse ate very sparingly. It was clear that she didn't like such simple food and was only taking a little of everything to be polite.

After the meal, the country mouse asked about life in the city, a place she had never seen. The town mouse talked for hours about the bright lights, the restaurants, the fine variety of mice in her sophisticated city. Afterward, they crept into a warm and lightly scented burrow in an old cedar log.

All night the country mouse dreamed of city life, with its new sights and sounds, tastes and smells. The next morning, when her friend asked her to come for a visit, the country mouse readily agreed.

Just after the dinner hour, they reached the imposing

mansion where the town mouse lived. The dining room was empty, but its long table was still piled high with ham, roast beef, steaming vegetables, mounded bowls of mashed potatoes, and plates of assorted cheeses and fruits.

The mice were eating their way across a plate of cheese slices when the cook entered the room. The two friends ran for the safety of the nearest mouse hole.

Once there, the country mouse turned to her city friend and said, "You certainly live in luxury, but I prefer my simple life, with its peace and security."

Moral: Peace and simplicity are better than the uproar caused by riches.

THE TRAVELERS
AND THE BEAR

wo merchants met at an inn just south of the great Forest of Mists. Each soon learned that the other was bound for the high-walled market town of Konigsberg, several days' journey north along the old Roman road. The forest had an evil reputation for bad weather, wild animals, and bold bandits, so the men decided to make their way through it together. They made a solemn pact to help one another in case of trouble.

Their trip was uneventful until the morning of the third day. Just as they were breaking camp, a huge black bear charged out of the dark forest.

One man ran for the nearest tree and swung up into its lower branches. From this vantage point he watched the other man drop to the ground and pretend to be dead.

The bear walked up to the man on the ground and sniffed all around his head, then he batted at the man's legs

with his front paws. After a few minutes, the bear wandered out of the camp.

The merchant in the tree climbed down and walked over to his companion, who was still so shaken that he couldn't get up.

"You must have had a very interesting conversation with that bear," he said, smiling broadly.

The man on the ground rolled over and sat up. "He is a very wise bear. He told me not to trust cowardly people like you to protect me."

Moral: The true strength of a friendship is only revealed by adversity.

THE TREES
AND THE AXE

A man strode into a forest one fall day with an axe head in his hand. "Oh, trees," he begged, "I need a small branch for a task I have in mind. It must be straight-grained and strong. If you could give me such a branch, I would be most obliged to all of you."

The trees were good natured, and the man struck them as charming and reasonable. They could think of no reason why they shouldn't oblige him. After consulting with each other, they offered the man a branch from an ash tree. As he had asked, the branch was straight-grained and strong. It contained no serious knots or other flaws.

"This is perfect!" the man exclaimed. "I will never forget your generosity." With that, he knelt down on the forest floor and quickly stripped the bark from the branch, sanded the wood, and fitted it into the axe head he carried. Taking a few

practice swings, he soon set to work cutting down tree after tree.

As their end approached, the trees realized the man had told them the truth. When he warmed himself by a fire built of logs from trunks, he would think of how they had helped him fix his axe. He would be obliged to them for providing him heat on a cold winter's night. Then the trees saw how foolish they had been in giving their enemy the weapon that would destroy them.

Moral: Foul intentions sometimes hide behind a reasonable request.

THE TWO
FROGS

ne summer the weather was unusually hot and dry. Weeks passed, and no rain fell. The lake in which two frogs lived started drying up. It began to look more like a pond. Then it became a mere mud hole. Finally the sun baked it dry. Even the water grasses and lily pads shriveled up.

The older frog said, "It is clear we cannot stay here any longer. We must venture out into the world and look for another lake. Deserts like this do not attract flies, and we need food. Besides, if we stay here much longer, our skin will dry up." The younger frog agreed, and soon the two frogs were on their way.

Hours passed, and the frogs did not discover any water. Knowing that birds could cover much more ground than they could, the frogs asked a crow perched on a branch if he had seen any water in his travels. "Over near that farm-

house," said the crow. "I saw sunlight reflecting, so there must be some water there."

Heartened by the crow's news, the two frogs hopped toward the farmhouse. Soon they discovered what the crow had seen. A stone wall surrounded a deep and deliciously cool well. Even the air was cooler around the water.

Seeing the water so tantalizingly near, the younger frog proposed that they jump in at once.

"Wait a bit," said the older frog. "If that well should dry up, how could we get out again?"

Moral: Look before you leap.

THE TWO
POTS

 uring heavy spring rains, a river overflowed its banks. It raced down streets and through houses and schools, snatching any objects it could carry away. Into the swift current whirled school desks, chairs, tables, couches, and even animals.

Among the items borne by the raging water were two pots. One was plain and made of earthenware, a kind of clay. The other was a heavy brass pot decorated with ornate patterns.

Although the pots came from different houses, the force of the water moved them closer to each other. Soon each pot could see the other clearly. Immediately the earthenware pot called over to the brass pot, "Please keep at a distance. Try not to come any closer, I beg of you."

"I'll be happy to oblige, if I can." said the brass pot, who was too self-confident to have hurt feelings."But what causes

you to make such a request? We've never met before, and as far as I know, I've never done you any harm. Why don't we work together? That way, we may be able to help each other survive this disaster."

"I'm sure you wouldn't intentionally cause me injury," the earthenware pot replied. "But you are so heavy and strong that if you bumped into me ever so slightly, I would smash into hundreds of pieces and sink into the mud at the bottom of this river. I am much more likely to survive this flood if you keep your distance."

Moral: Beware of casual acquaintances. Although they may mean no harm, they can cause permanent damage.

THE TWO
RABBITS

rabbit about to have a family pleaded with another rabbit for the use of her hutch. "I am going to have a large number of babies," she said, sniffing, her eyes filled with tears. "And I have nowhere to keep them safely. What a tragedy it would be to see my own children eaten by a fox."

Her friend comforted her and readily agreed to let the rabbit use her hutch. She even insisted that the expectant mother move in at once. Days passed, and the rabbit gave birth to a large number of healthy rabbits.

When the time came for the mother rabbit and her babies to move out, the owner of the hutch stopped by and gently suggested that the family leave so that she could once again live in her home.

The mother rabbit replied, "I am truly sorry to have kept you so long. My little ones are still weak, and I worry that they aren't yet ready to fend for themselves. Could we have

your hutch for another two weeks? I'm sure you wouldn't want to hear of the death of one of my babies and know that you could have prevented it."

The hutch's owner agreed, but when the two weeks were up, she said to the mother rabbit, "You and your babies must leave now."

"Must!" exclaimed the mother rabbit. "We'll see about that! Unless you can defeat me and all my young, you will never have this hutch again."

Moral: Possession is nine points of the law.

THE VAIN
JACKDAW

upiter decided to select a sovereign who would rule over all the other birds. He issued a proclamation declaring that at sunrise in six days, the birds should meet with him. He would then decide which of them was the most beautiful and would crown that bird king over the other birds.

When the jackdaw read Jupiter's proclamation, he at first despaired of having any chance of being crowned king. He was honest enough to realize that many creatures found his black-and-gray feathers dull. His raucous call, like two branches creaking together in the wind, didn't add to his appeal. The jackdaw knew all too well that most birds thought he was the ugliest bird ever born.

But the jackdaw was also ambitious. He set his mind to coming up with a way to hide his ugly appearance. Suddenly he knew the answer. During the next five days, he searched the woods, collecting all the beautiful feathers that had fallen

from the wings of other birds. The night before Jupiter's meeting, the jackdaw stuck his collection of feathers all over his body.

That morning as the sun rose, all the birds assembled before Jupiter. After inspecting the birds, Jupiter proposed that the jackdaw be crowned king. The other birds indignantly protested. So upset were they, that they flew at the jackdaw and plucked their old feathers from him. When they were done, it was clear to all that the once beautiful bird was merely an ordinary jackdaw.

Moral: Borrowed feathers do not make fine birds.

THE VINE AND THE GOAT

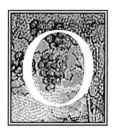ne hot day in late summer, a young white goat wandered aimlessly through a vineyard. He noticed a grapevine heavy with ripening grapes and thick with succulent leaves. Several hours had passed since the goat had left the barnyard, and he was quite hungry and thirsty. Without thinking beyond his own need for food and drink, he stopped and tore at the tender shoots of the vine. They were sweet and juicy. The goat continued chewing away, ripping through leaves, grapes, and tendrils until he was no longer hungry and his thirst was quenched.

Shaking his head in satisfaction, he was turning to go when a clear voice rang out. Startled, the goat looked around to locate the speaker. To his surprise, the voice came from the ruined and ragged grapevine.

"I will revenge myself on you," the vine trumpeted, its voice strong in spite of its wounds. "You have injured me

without cause. Couldn't you have satisfied your hunger by eating the young tender grass? Yet you thoughtlessly damaged my leaves and threatened my life."

"But even if you had chewed me down to my roots," the vine continued, "I'd have the satisfaction of knowing your fate. Before the snow falls, you will be taken to the altar to be sacrificed. Once you are tied up and placed on the altar, the priest will pour wine from my grapes all over you. My wine will be the dew of death, and your last thought will be sorrow for how badly you treated me."

Moral: Though sometimes delayed, retribution will come.

THE VIPER
AND THE FILE

frustrated viper—a venomous, slithering red-
dish-brown fellow—was having no luck find-
ing any food to eat. No matter how still he lay
in wait, no matter how well he disguised himself against the stones of the field, every mouse or toad or
other little creature that happened by escaped him. As a field
mouse at last headed straight toward him, the shadow of a
huge hawk sent both viper and mouse fleeing for safety. The
world is surely against me the viper thought.

He had gone for days without eating. His stomach felt
hollow, and he grew weaker every hour. In desperation, he
headed to a smith's shop. The building was terribly hot
because of the roaring fire in the forge. The viper could feel
his skin drying up and flaking away with each moment he
lingered, but he was certain he would find a mouse some-
where in the room.

No matter how hard the viper looked, he couldn't find a living thing to eat. Even the smith had left the shop to get a cool drink at the well. Driven by rage and despair, the viper charged at a metal file and chomped down on it with the little strength he had left.

Chuckling, the file said, "Your energy would be better spent looking for food elsewhere. You aren't likely to get much of a meal from me because I am designed to bite wood and metal, not to be chewed on by others."

Moral: It's madness to lash out in anger with the intention of hurting another, for in truth we only wound ourselves.

THE WANTON
CALF

A calf didn't have a care in the world. All day he stampeded through the fields with other calves and drank from clear streams whenever he wished. When he felt tired, he collapsed on the cool grass and fell asleep as the sun's rays warmed his back.

One day he noticed a sturdy ox yoked to a plough. The ox trudged through a nearby field, working hard to turn over the soil. The thoughtless calf couldn't resist taunting the ox. "What a poor drudge you are," he teased. "See what a happy life I lead. I go where I please and drink at the best streams and thoroughly enjoy myself. You, however, must work in this field and do whatever the farmer commands. Don't you wish you could enjoy the leisurely life I have?"

The ox ignored the calf's words and quietly continued his work. Bored because he wasn't getting any reaction, the calf soon trotted off to join his friends in their games.

That evening, the ox was unyoked and turned loose in the field. A few moments later, he saw the calf taken out of the field and delivered to the priest, who led him away to be sacrificed.

Just before the knife plunged into the calf's throat, the ox drew near and whispered, "Look at how your leisurely life ends. You were allowed to live only so that you could be sacrificed. Tell me, carefree calf, whose life would you rather have now?"

Moral: Ignore the words of a fool. They lead to death.

THE WASPS AND THE HONEY POT

A swarm of wasps was out looking for food one warm summer morning. The wasps were used to having to fly from flower to flower, working hard all day to gather enough nectar to eat. Life was difficult, but no wasps complained. They reasoned it was better than no life at all.

When one of the wasps buzzed in excitement, the others flew near to see what had him in such a tizzy. He had discovered some honey pots. One pot was partly uncovered, and the wasps could smell the honey's sweet scent wafting up to them,

The leader of the wasps flew in to investigate. Sure enough, he confirmed, here was enough honey to feed their entire hive for days. When the news reached wasps farther away, they flew in to join the excited, buzzing swarm. Many wasps flew into the pot and began eating their fill.

Some wasps flew back to the hive to spread the word about their discovery. The wasps in the hive followed their mates to the honey pot and squeezed their way inside. Everyone was having so much fun eating the honey that at first they didn't notice how crowded the pot was getting.

When all the wasps had finally eaten their fill and were ready to leave the honey pot, they discovered that they were packed in so tightly they couldn't escape. Only when it was too late did they realize that some pleasures cost too much.

Moral: Greediness brings its own punishment.

THE WOLF AND
THE CRANE

ravenous wolf gobbled down his kill so quickly that he got a bone stuck in his throat. No
matter how he tried, he couldn't swallow that
bone. He thought of stuffing his paws down
his throat to pry the bone out, but his paws were too big.

The wolf was in tremendous pain. Even swallowing
water was difficult, and he feared that he would soon die of
hunger or thirst. So the wolf hurried through the fields and
woods, begging every animal he met to remove the bone
from his throat. He realized that not many animals would be
anxious to help a wolf, so he promised a huge reward to any-
one who would ease his pain. For days and nights he traveled
across the land, finding no one who dared to accept his offer.

At last a crane, moved by pity and the promise of a
reward, undertook the dangerous task. He carefully threaded
his long beak down the wolf's mouth and grabbed the bone.
Gingerly wiggling the bone first one way and then another,

the crane managed to dislodge it and pulled it from the wolf's throat. The wolf leaped with joy, jubilant that his problem had been solved.

"Before you go," said the crane, "there is one more thing to take care of. You need to give me my reward."

"Wretch," said the wolf. "You should be grateful that when you put your head in my mouth, I didn't bite it off."

Moral: When dealing with dangerous people, the best reward is to come away from the experience safely.

THE WOLF AND
THE DONKEY

O ne early spring day, a donkey was grazing in a meadow when he caught the sound of something stalking him. Glancing around, he caught sight of a half-starved wolf. Obviously the winter had been hard on this wolf, whose ribs showed clearly through his thin coat, and he was hoping to make a meal of the donkey.

The donkey knew danger when he saw it, even weak and half starved. He seized on a plan and began to limp around the meadow, pretending he could barely walk.

The wolf grew curious. Instead of attacking the donkey, he trotted up to him and asked what had happened to make him so lame.

"I was pushing my way through a hedge," the donkey explained, "and didn't notice a large thorn on the ground. I stepped right on it. It cut deep into my hoof, and there it stays." The donkey sighed.

He looked at the wolf and said, "I realize you want to make a meal of me, but before you do, perhaps you should remove that thorn so that it doesn't injure your throat when you are eating."

"How thoughtful of you to care about my comfort at such at time," the wolf said. "Here. Let me lift your foot and get at that thorn."

As soon as the wolf began lifting the donkey's foot, the donkey kicked his teeth out and galloped away. The wolf, badly hurt, said, "This serves me right. My father taught me to be a butcher, not a doctor."

Moral: We are better off when we do what we are trained for.

THE WOLF
AND THE LAMB

ne fine summer day, a wolf ambled down to a
stream and began to drink. Glancing up, he
spied a young lamb who was just beginning to
drink from a little lower down the stream. The
wolf examined the lamb carefully. She was plump and
healthy. His mouth watered as he thought of how tender that
lamb would taste. His rumbling stomach reminded the wolf
that he hadn't eaten anything all day. There's my supper,
thought the wolf, if I can only find some excuse for killing
her.

After a moment's thought, he called out to the lamb,
"How dare you muddy the water I am drinking?"

"You are mistaken," said the lamb. "I cannot muddy your
water, because the stream runs past you before it reaches
me."

"Well then," said the wolf, "I remember how you called

me bad names last year. You embarrassed me in front of another wolf. That is an insult I have never forgiven."

"That cannot be," protested the lamb. "I am only six months old."

"Well, if it was not you, then it was certainly your father," declared the wolf. "I never forget a face, and your resemblance to him is stunning." His eyes turned fierce. Without another word he raced down the edge of the stream and seized the lamb by the throat.

As she died, the lamb gasped out, "Any excuse suits a tyrant."

Moral: Those who want to do wrong will find an excuse to justify their actions.

The Wolf
as Piper

herd of goats was grazing in a field. One young goat was tired of playing games with his friends. He always won the bucking contests and could leap higher than any of the other young goats. He wanted something new to do so he decided to explore the far end of the field. He was quite a distance from the safety of the herd and the dogs who protected it when he spotted a wolf stalking him.

Turning around to face the wolf, the kid said, "I know, friend wolf, that you intend to eat me. But out of the goodness of your heart, before I die, grant me one favor. Play me a tune on these pipes someone has dropped here, so that I can have one last dance."

Seeing no harm in the request and willing to humor the young goat before he killed it, the wolf played a cheerful tune on the pipes, and the kid danced. So entertained was the wolf by the kid's dance that he didn't notice that the

dogs who were guarding the goats had heard the music as well. They raced to investigate and charged at the wolf.

Throwing the pipes down, the wolf took to his heels and headed for the forest. Once he had reached safety, he muttered, "This is what happens when people go meddling in work that is not their profession. My job was to play the butcher, not the piper."

Moral: He who plays the fool generally misses the prize.

The Wolf In Sheep's Clothing

A wolf decided he was tired of having to hunt every day simply to have enough to eat. He figured that there had to be an easier way to get along in the world. When he asked other wolves if they had any ideas of how to make hunting easier, they laughed at him. "This is the way it has always been, and the way it will always be," they said.

But the wolf was not convinced. During long moonlit nights when he was off by himself, he tried to think of a new approach to hunting. Finally he had an idea. He decided to disguise himself by wearing a sheepskin and sneaking in with a flock of sheep.

The next day he put his plan into action. He killed a large sheep and treated its hide. Then he dressed himself in his new coat and snuck into a flock of sheep at dawn, thinking that the dim light would make it more difficult for the shepherd to notice.

The wolf succeeded better than he had hoped. He spent the rest of the day grazing with the sheep and looking forward to nighttime, when he would so easily eat his fill of mutton and lamb.

As the moon rose, the shepherd shut the wolf up with the sheep in the barn and locked the door. Then he changed his mind and unlocked it. The shepherd wanted some lamb for his supper, mistook the wolf for a sheep, and killed him on the spot.

Moral: Those who lay traps are often caught by their own bait.

FURTHER READINGS

Caduto, Michael J. *Earth Tales from Around the World*. Golden, Colo.: Fulcrum, 1997.

Creedon, Sharon. *Fair is Fair: World Folktales of Justice*. Little Rock, Ark.: August House, 1997.

Czernecki, Stefan. *The Cricket's Cage: A Chinese Folktale*. New York: Hyperion, 1997.

Goble, Paul. *Iktomi and the Buzzard: A Plains Indian Story*. New York: Orchard, 1994.

Gonzalez, Lucia M. *The Bossy Gallito: A Traditional Cuban Folk Tale*. New York: Scholastic, 1994.

Han, Suzanne Crowder. *The Rabbit's Judgment*. New York: Holt, 1994.

London, Jonathan. *What Newt Could Do for Turtle*. Cambridge, Mass.: Candlewick, 1996.

Martin, Rafe, ed. *Mysterious Tales of Japan*. New York: Putnam, 1996.

Mayo, Margaret. *When the World Was Young: Creation and Pourquois Tales*. New York: Simon & Schuster, 1996.

Reneaux, J. J. *Why Alligator Hates Dog: A Cajun Folktale*. Little Rock, Ark.: August House, 1995.

Ross, Gale. *How Turtle's Back Was Cracked: A Traditional Cherokee Tale*. New York: Dial, 1995.

Roth, Susan L. *The Biggest Frog in Australia*. New York: Simon & Schuster, 1996.

Voake, Charlotte. *Ginger*. Cambridge, Mass.: Candlewick, 1997.

Walking Turtle, Eagle. *Full Moon Stories: Thirteen Native American Legends*. New York: Hyperion, 1997.

INDEX ❡

BRUCE and BECKY DUROST FISH are freelance writers and editors who have worked on more than one hundred books for children and young adults. They have degrees in history and literature and live in the high desert of Central Oregon.